WILD WHEELS
FERRARIS

By Bob Power

Gareth Stevens
Publishing

Please visit our website, www.garethstevens.com. For a free color catalog of all our high-quality books, call toll free 1-800-542-2595 or fax 1-877-542-2596.

Library of Congress Cataloging-in-Publication Data

Power, Bob, 1959-
  Ferraris / Bob Power.
    p. cm. — (Wild wheels)
  Includes index.
  ISBN 978-1-4339-5828-1 (pbk.)
  ISBN 978-1-4339-5829-8 (6-pack)
  ISBN 978-1-4339-5826-7 (library binding)
  1. Ferrari automobile—History—Juvenile literature. I. Title.
  TL215.F47P692 2012
  629.222—dc22

2011000514

First Edition

Published in 2012 by
Gareth Stevens Publishing
111 East 14th Street, Suite 349
New York, NY 10003

Copyright © 2012 Gareth Stevens Publishing

Designer: Daniel Hosek
Editor: Kristen Rajczak

Photo credits: Cover, backgrounds (cover and interior pages), pp. 1, 4–5 (all images), 6–7, 8–9 (all images) Shutterstock.com; p. 5 (Ferrari logo) Bloomberg/Getty Images; p. 7 (Enzo Ferrari) Evening Standard/Getty Images; pp. 10–11, 18–19 Car Culture/Getty Images; pp. 12–13 Dave M. Benett/Getty Images; pp. 14–15 Mike Hewitt/Getty Images; pp. 16–17 Oli Scarff/Getty Images; pp. 20–21, 22–23 Cameron Spencer/Getty Images; p. 23 (458 Italia) David Livingston/Getty Images; pp. 24–25 Clive Mason/Getty Images; pp. 26–27 Juergen Schwarz/Getty Images; pp. 28–29 Miguel Medina/AFP/Getty Images.

Printed in the United States of America

CPSIA compliance information: Batch #CS11GS: For further information contact Gareth Stevens, New York, New York at 1-800-542-2595.

CONTENTS

Words in the glossary appear in **bold** type the first time they are used in the text.

Power and Grace

Ferraris are among the coolest and best-loved cars in the world. These cars are known for being stylish—and expensive. However, a Ferrari's most important feature is its speed. Every Ferrari is **designed** to be fast. For example, the Enzo Ferrari can exceed an astonishing 218 miles (350 km) per hour!

Ferraris have a special logo that's easy to recognize. It's a black **"prancing"** horse standing on one back foot with its other feet in the air. The logo fits the cars the Ferrari company makes. Just like a racehorse, a Ferrari is beautiful and fast.

The horse in the Ferarri logo is on a yellow rectangle with rounded corners. It used to be on a shield. The top of the rectangle has red, white, and green stripes. These are the colors of the Italian flag.

This Ferrari F430 can reach 195 miles (314 km) per hour!

Enzo Ferrari

The Ferrari company was formed by Enzo Ferrari. He was born in 1898 in Modena, Italy. Enzo's parents were Alfredo and Adalgisa Ferrari. His father owned a company that made metal parts. Enzo had one brother, Alfredo Jr. When Enzo was 10, his father took the brothers to a car race in Bologna, Italy. From that time on, Enzo loved car racing.

This car was named after the Ferrari company's founder. It's called the Enzo.

Enzo had a happy childhood, but sad times followed. His father and brother died in 1916. Soon after, Enzo joined the army. At this time, Italy was fighting in World War I. In 1918, Enzo caught **influenza** and nearly died. When he got better, he was let out of the army.

Enzo Ferrari

INSIDE THE MACHINE

Enzo didn't like school much as a boy, but he enjoyed many outdoor activities. He loved riding bicycles. He also liked hunting. Enzo and his brother owned pigeons that they entered in pigeon races.

Racing Cars

Once he left the army, Enzo Ferrari looked for a job. However, many other soldiers were looking for work after the war, too. At last, Ferrari found a job testing cars for a carmaker called CMN. In the following years, he took up car racing.

In 1923, Ferrari won a race called the Circuito del Savio. This brought him to the attention of the Count and Countess Baracca, whose son had been Italy's greatest flying ace during World War I. They were so struck by Ferrari's skill that they suggested he use the horse logo their son had used on his planes.

INSIDE THE MACHINE

The count and countess's son, Francesco Baracca, was an ace pilot. An ace is a pilot who has shot down many enemy planes in a war. Baracca shot down 34 planes. He died in 1918 after his own plane was shot down.

Ferrari still puts the old shield logo on some cars.

The Scuderia Ferrari

In 1929, Enzo Ferrari formed a racing team called the Scuderia Ferrari. Most of its cars came from the Italian carmaker Alfa Romeo. Ferrari began working with Alfa Romeo on car designs. In 1938, Alfa Romeo took over the Scuderia Ferrari. Ferrari worked there until starting his own race-car company in 1939. It grew slowly during World War II.

This 1947 Ferrari is one of the first race cars Ferrari built.

After the war, Ferrari designed the car that would become the first official Ferrari. It was powered by a V-12 engine—one with 12 **cylinders** arranged in two banks angled in a V shape. The car was built in 1947. It became known as the Ferrari 125 S.

INSIDE THE MACHINE

"Scuderia" means "stable" in Italian. Just as a certain stable is home to a famous group of racehorses, Ferrari hoped his club would be home to a famous group of race cars. The name also called to mind Ferrari's horse logo.

Introducing the GT

In 1949, the Ferrari company introduced its first car that was meant to be driven on the road rather than the racetrack. It was called the Ferrari 166 Inter. It was the company's first GT. "GT" stands for *gran turismo,* which is the Italian term for "grand touring" or "grand tourer." These cars traveled longer distances than the cars built for racing could travel.

Ferrari's GTs, like this Ferrari 250 GT, have been popular for more than 60 years.

The 166 Inter was first shown to the public at the Paris Motor Show in October 1949. It became the first in a long line of GTs made by Ferrari. These cars had two seats and a V-12 engine just like the 125 S.

INSIDE THE MACHINE

The 166 Inter was a big hit. However, Enzo Ferrari only started selling cars that could be driven on a normal road to earn money to make his race cars. In fact, he often complained about the people buying his cars!

A Growing Company

Over the years, Ferrari came out with many new cars. The company tried to make each model better than the one that had come before it. In 1960, Ferrari came out with its first 2+2 car. This is a car with two seats up front and two in the back.

CLUB ITALIA

In 1962, the company introduced the Ferrari 250 GTO. It was an extrapowerful GT. Its body was **aerodynamic**. At that time, races for cars that were not built just for the track were popular. The GTO was built to take part in these races. It won many!

Fewer than forty 250 GTOs were produced, and many of the ones that still exist no longer have their original engine or body.

INSIDE THE MACHINE

Enzo Ferrari said that his father, Alfredo, was a big fan of the 2+2 cars. Alfredo Ferrari always had his dog and another person in the car with him when he drove. The 2+2 provided room for everyone to sit comfortably.

15

The Dino

In 1968, Ferrari introduced a new car called the Dino 206 GT. It was the first in a line of Dinos. Dinos were less expensive than other Ferraris. They had smaller, less powerful engines, too. The first Dinos had V-6 engines, or engines with 6 cylinders. Later models of the Dino used V-8 engines.

While the engines in earlier Ferrari road cars were in the front of the car, the engines in Dinos were in the middle of the car. Cars designed like this are known as mid-engine cars. Several winning race cars designed by the race-car wing of the Ferrari company had been mid-engine cars.

Enzo Ferrari's son, Alfredo, was nicknamed Dino. Dino helped design V-6 engines for Ferrari race cars. Sadly, Dino died in 1956. The Ferrari Dino was named to honor his memory.

Dinos like this one were made from 1968 to 1976.

Berlinetta Boxers and Testarossas

Mid-engine cars are fast and powerful. However, the Dino's smaller engine kept it from being more powerful than V-12 Ferraris. In 1973, Ferrari began selling its first mid-engine car with a 12-cylinder engine. The car was called the Berlinetta Boxer. The Boxer had a flat-12 engine. This means its 12 cylinders were set up in a flat line, unlike the V-12. The **pistons** in the engine moved back and forth instead of up and down.

The Testarossa was a more traditional Ferrari than the Dino. It was fast and flashy!

In 1984, the Berlinetta Boxer was replaced by the Testarossa. It was more aerodynamic than the Berlinetta Boxer and provided a more comfortable ride.

INSIDE THE MACHINE

At first, the Testarossa's new look surprised people. Its rear wheels were wider than its front wheels. Deep cuts on the car's sides took in air to help cool the engine. Most people liked the way the car drove, though, and it was a big success.

The Enzo

Enzo Ferrari designed and oversaw the design of many great cars during his long life. He died on August 14, 1988, at the age of 90. The last car designed under him was the Ferrari F40. Like the GTO before it, the F40 was built for the track but could also be driven on a normal road. When it first came out, it was the fastest car around!

Owners of the Enzo must use a certain kind of oil in their cars and follow other rules set by Ferrari. If they don't, they might not be able to buy another Ferrari in the future.

After Ferrari's death, the company kept producing great cars. In 2003, it made the Enzo Ferrari. The Enzo was suited to both the track and the road. It had a newly designed 660-**horsepower** V-12 engine.

INSIDE THE MACHINE

Fewer than 400 Enzo Ferraris were made. Drivers had to apply to the company to become an owner. Not only did they have to pay for the car, but they also had to promise to follow the rules Ferrari set for owners.

The California

Ferrari introduced the Ferrari California in 2008. It was the first Ferrari with a V-8 engine located in a mid-front position. It reached speeds of 193 miles (310 km) per hour. The California was also the company's first hardtop **convertible**.

The newly designed engine was the first to use direct fuel **injection**. When car engines burn fuel inside their cylinders, the fuel

The Ferrari California wowed onlookers at the 2008 Australian International Motor Show.

needs to be mixed with air. In a direct-fuel-injection engine, the air and gas are mixed inside the cylinder, not in a separate **chamber**. This saves gas, pollutes the air less, and creates more power.

INSIDE THE MACHINE

Ferrari followed up the California with the 2010 Ferrari 458 Italia. The car produced 570 horsepower. It had a wedge-shaped body with carefully placed air vents. This kept it from being slowed down by air as it zipped along.

458 Italia

Formula 1 Winners

Though many of the best-known and best-loved Ferraris were built for the road, the company was founded to build race cars. Many of them have been winners, too! Like Enzo Ferrari's early racing team, the part of the company that designs race cars is called Scuderia Ferrari.

Many Ferrari race cars have been built for a kind of racing known as Formula 1, or F1. The company won its first F1 race in 1951. From 2000 through 2004, driver Michael Schumacher won the F1 world championship every year for Ferrari.

INSIDE THE MACHINE

Ferrari has had many great F1 drivers over the years. In 1952, Alberto Ascari became the first Ferrari driver to win the F1 world championship. He won again the next year! Ferrari driver Niki Lauda also won the F1 world championship twice, in 1975 and 1977.

Michael Schumacher drives a Ferrari in the 2004 F1 Brazilian **Grand Prix**.

That's a Ferrari!

Ferraris are beautiful and fast. They're also one of the most expensive sports cars around. Many people over the years have dreamed of owning a Ferrari. For car lovers, a Ferrari gives its owner high-class **status**.

Like many Ferraris, this Ferrari 275 GTB SN is a classic!

Ferraris have been used in movies and TV shows. They show up in the movies *Cars*, *Ferris Bueller's Day Off*, and *Gone in 60 Seconds*. The hero of the TV show *Magnum, P.I.* drove his boss's red Ferrari 308 GTS. One of the main characters on the TV show *Miami Vice* drove a Ferrari. The company even supplied a Testarossa to be used on the show.

INSIDE THE MACHINE

A 2011 Ferrari costs between $192,000 and $450,000. However, Ferraris from the 1960s can cost millions of dollars!

Future Ferraris

Interest in Ferraris remains strong around the world. The company's museum in Maranello, Italy, gets more than 200,000 visitors each year. In 2010, a Ferrari theme park called Ferrari World opened in Abu Dhabi, in the United Arab Emirates. The park is home to the world's fastest roller coaster, the Formula Rossa.

Ferrari introduced the Aperta at the Paris Motor Show in 2010.

In 2010, Ferrari introduced a new car called the Ferrari 599 SA Aperta. It's an open car with a 670-horsepower engine. Whatever changes await future Ferraris, one thing is certain: They're going to be fast!

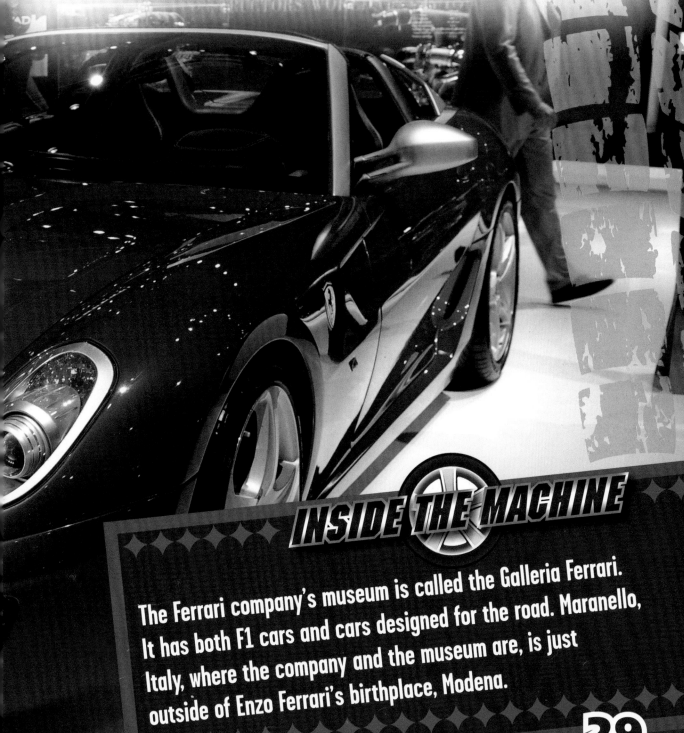

INSIDE THE MACHINE

The Ferrari company's museum is called the Galleria Ferrari. It has both F1 cars and cars designed for the road. Maranello, Italy, where the company and the museum are, is just outside of Enzo Ferrari's birthplace, Modena.

Glossary

aerodynamic: having a shape that improves airflow around a car to increase its speed

chamber: an enclosed space

convertible: a car with a roof that can be lowered or removed

cylinder: the enclosed spaces for pistons in an engine

design: to create the pattern or shape of something

grand prix: the name used for an F1 race. It is French for "grand prize."

horsepower: the measurement of an engine's power

influenza: a sickness that can include fever, upset stomach, and aches and pains; also known as the flu

injection: to introduce something forcefully

piston: a piece in an engine that slides up and down inside the cylinder as it makes power for the engine

prance: to move in a spirited way by springing from the back legs

status: a position or rank

For More Information

Books

Aloian, Molly. *Ferrari*. New York, NY: Crabtree Publishing Company, 2011.

Hawley, Rebecca. *Ferrari*. New York, NY: PowerKids Press, 2007.

Websites

F1: Ferrari
www.formula1.com/teams_and_drivers/teams/3/
Find out more about the Scuderia Ferrari Marlboro and their record over the years.

Ferrari
www.ferrari.com
Learn more about the Ferrari company and its cars. Read about Enzo Ferrari's life.

Ferrari World
www.ferrariworldabudhabi.com
Explore the rides and events at Ferrari World.

Index